WORLD CELEBRATIONS

JUNETEENTH

KATHRYN WALTON

Published in 2026 by The Rosen Publishing Group, Inc.
2544 Clinton Street, Buffalo, NY 14224

Copyright © 2026 by The Rosen Publishing Group, Inc.

All rights reserved. No part of this book may be reproduced in any form without permission in writing from the publisher, except by a reviewer.

First Edition

Editor: Greg Roza
Book Design: Rachel Rising

Photo Credits: Cover, p. 1 Hamara/Shutterstock.com; pp. 4, 6, 8, 10, 12, 14, 16, 18, 20 Vjom/Shutterstock.com; p. 5 Raymond Abercrombie/iStock.com; p. 7 https://commons.wikimedia.org/wiki/File:Battle_of_Franklin,_November_30,_1864.jpg; p. 9 https://en.wikipedia.org/wiki/File:Lincoln_O-17_by_Brady,_1860.png; p. 11 https://commons.wikimedia.org/wiki/File:Emancipation_Day_in_Richmond,_Virginia,_1905.jpg; p. 13 hlphoto/Shutterstock.com; p. 13 DyrElena/Shutterstock.com; p. 15 Wirestock Creators/Shutterstock.com; p. 17 Max kegfire/Shutterstock.com; p. 19 Alexis K Grimsley/Shutterstock.com; p. 21 SeventyFour/Shutterstock.com.

Some of the images in this book illustrate individuals who are models. The depictions do not imply actual situations or events.

Cataloging-in-Publication Data

Names: Walton, Kathryn, 1993-.
Title: Juneteenth / Kathryn Walton.
Description: Buffalo, New York : PowerKids Press, 2026. | Series: World celebrations | Includes glossary and index.
Identifiers: ISBN 9781499452150 (pbk.) | ISBN 9781499452167 (library bound) | ISBN 9781499452174 (ebook)
Subjects: LCSH: Juneteenth–Juvenile literature. | African Americans–Texas–History–Juvenile literature. | Enslaved persons–Emancipation–United States–Juvenile literature. | African Americans–Anniversaries, etc.–Juvenile literature.
Classification: LCC E185.93.T4 W367 2026 | DDC 394.263–dc23

Manufactured in the United States of America

CPSIA Compliance Information: Batch #CSPK26. For Further Information contact Rosen Publishing at 1-800-237-9932.

CONTENTS

An American Holiday 4

The American Civil War 6

Through the Years 10

Let's Eat! 12

Fun for All 14

A Day of Service 16

What Is Activism? 18

Remembering the Past 20

Glossary 22

For More Infomation 23

Index. 24

An American Holiday

Juneteenth is short for June Nineteenth. It is a celebration that started in Texas in 1865. It honors the day when **enslaved people** in Texas learned that they had been given their freedom. Juneteenth has grown over the years. It is a holiday all Americans can celebrate!

The American Civil War

In the 1860s, Americans from the North and Americans from the South had a war. It is called the American Civil War. The biggest problem between the two was **slavery**. Many southern farms still used enslaved people as workers. Many northern people wanted to stop slavery. This led to war.

The American Civil War came to an end in 1865. This was partly because of the leadership of President Abraham Lincoln. In 1863, Lincoln wrote a special **document** that said all enslaved people in the South were now free. Enslaved people in Texas didn't know this until 1865.

Through the Years

Early Juneteenth celebrations began around 1866. They were mainly among Black church communities in Texas. As freed enslaved people and their families moved all over the United States, they took their Juneteenth **traditions** with them. Juneteenth became an official American holiday in 2021.

11

Let's Eat!

Juneteenth celebrations often have big feasts! Barbecued, or grilled, meats are common. People eat steaks, ribs, hotdogs, and hamburgers. Sweet treats such as pies and cakes are common too. Many foods served for Juneteenth are red. The red color stands for the blood of people enslaved long ago.

Fun for All

Juneteenth **festivals** take place all over the country every June. Celebrations may have parades, neighborhood parties, and **fireworks**. People listen to live music, dance, eat, and have fun! Many organized celebrations take place in parks or other public places. Some people choose to celebrate with friends and family.

A Day of Service

To some, Juneteenth is a day of service to help others in the community. This could mean helping at a local animal shelter. You could ask an older person in your neighborhood if they need any help. You could raise money for a cause you like.

What Is Activism?

Activism means trying to make changes in your community. On Juneteenth, some people teach others about problems that still hurt Americans. This could be problems between Black and white people. It could be about keeping the **environment** safe. Crowds listen to people speak about topics that affect every American.

Remembering the Past

Juneteenth is a time for remembering America's past and the people who lived under slavery. It is a day to celebrate freedom and to teach others about American history. Many people who honor the holiday tell stories from the past. Juneteenth reminds us how important freedom is.

GLOSSARY

document: An official piece of writing.

enslaved person: Someone forced to work for others for no pay.

environment: The natural world around us.

festival: A time of celebration in honor of something or someone special.

fireworks: A display of explosions and light high in the air created by the burning of chemicals.

slavery: The practice of forcing people to work without pay.

tradition: A way of thinking, behaving, or doing something that's been used by people in a particular group for a long time.

FOR MORE INFORMATION

BOOKS

Keppeler, Jill. *20 Fun Facts About Juneteenth*. New York, NY: Gareth Stevens Publishing, 2024.

Wynter, Anne. *So Many Years: A Juneteenth Story*. New York, NY: HarperCollins, 2025.

WEBSITES

Celebrating Juneteenth

kids.nationalgeographic.com/history/article/celebrating-juneteenth

Learn more about the history and traditions of Juneteenth.

History of Juneteenth

www.juneteenth.com/history

This detailed website has more to say about the history and traditions of Juneteenth.

Publisher's note to educators and parents: Our editors have carefully reviewed these websites to ensure that they are suitable for students. Many websites change frequently, however, and we cannot guarantee that a site's future contents will continue to meet our high standards of quality and educational value. Be advised that students should be closely supervised whenever they access the internet.

INDEX

A
activism, 18
American Civil War, 4, 6, 8

C
community, 16, 18

E
enslaved people, 4, 8, 10, 12

F
families, 10, 14
festivals, 14

foods, 12
freedom, 4, 20

L
Lincoln, Abraham, 8

M
music, 14

S
slavery, 6, 20

T
traditions, 10
Texas, 4, 8, 10